*The Rose Garden*

Books by Otto Friedrich

The
Rose Garden

by

OTTO FRIEDRICH

J. B. LIPPINCOTT COMPANY
Philadelphia and New York

U.S. Library of Congress Cataloging in Publication Data

Friedrich, Otto, birth date
    The rose garden.

    Autobiographical.
    1. Rose culture. I. Title.
SB411.F75   635.933′372   70–37926
ISBN–0–397–00854–6

The material in this book was originally published in shorter form in *McCall's* under the title "I Promised Myself a Rose Garden."

Lines from "Burnt Norton" and "Little Gidding" in *Four Quartets* by T. S. Eliot are quoted by permission of Harcourt Brace Jovanovich, Inc.

To Priscilla

1.

Footfalls in the memory

In the summer of my fortieth year, I suddenly decided one day that I wanted to create a rose garden. I had never before had any particular interest in roses—or gardening in general—and I had never even seen anything worthy of my image of a rose garden. And yet there ran through my mind, on this summer day, the lines that occur near the beginning of "Burnt Norton":

> Footfalls echo in the memory
> Down the passage which we did not take
> Towards the door we never opened
> Into the rose-garden. . . .

I have no idea why lines like that become embedded in the memory, but occasionally it happens. There was a time several years ago when I had to weed a strawberry patch, and I was driven gradually to the edge of madness by the sound of a voice inside my head, repeating endlessly the exhortation of Chairman Mao: "Let a hundred flowers blossom, let a hundred schools of thought contend." Now, haunted by Eliot's lines, I wanted not just a few roses but a rose garden, a place isolated from the lawn and the tulips and the peonies, dedicated entirely to roses. On the other hand, I had neither the energy nor the inclination to plan a vast arboretum—or even, knowing nothing about the subject, to learn the basic rules for growing roses.

I simply went to a local nursery and bought two rosebushes that attracted my eye—a white one named John F. Kennedy and a dark red one named Oklahoma. I dug two holes in an open space in the oak forest outside my house, and then I planted the two rosebushes and left them to fend for themselves. This procedure was not as aleatory as it might seem. The two rosebushes stood alone in a small clearing strewn with oak leaves, but the whole process of gardening is based, I think, on a series of visions. And here, in Locust Valley, at the top of a sandy hill just a few hundred yards inland from the lapping edge of Long Island Sound, I envisioned a citadel of roses, a fortress of tranquillity.

Visions do not create themselves, however. In some way, the idea of a rose garden, and the echoing recollection of the lines from "Burnt Norton," evolved from a kind of internal crisis I had undergone two years earlier. To state it in the simplest terms, I had gradually become convinced that I was going to die, and quite soon, and that there was nothing whatever I could do about it. There was no particular reason for this obsession—it may even be quite common, for all I know, among men in their late thirties—but the lack of a reason did not make its narcotic effect any less powerful.

For six months or so, I waited stoically for death to come—announced by one of those inevitable modern heralds, the chest X ray or the electrocardiogram—and then I decided, while waiting, that I would like to take my wife on one last trip back to Europe. And so we set out to revisit some of the places where we had lived in our youth, and to see some of the famous sights that we had been too snobbishly ignorant to look at before. We drove through the jagged mountains of Wales, we inspected the houses of Parliament, we climbed the windy towers of Notre Dame, we stood in the darkness beneath the rose window of Chartres. We watched the giant carp leaping from the pond at Fontainebleau, and the string orchestra playing waltzes at the Ritz Hotel in Madrid, and the bulls lurching to their doom at Aranjuez. And all of this filled me with an emotion I had never really experienced before, a sense of great joy in being alive. The pall that had hung over me for the past year, the premonition of impending death, simply faded away.

I do not know how or why this renewed enjoyment of life eventually led to my starting a rose garden, but it did.

2.

M*ary poppins*

Before I started my rose garden, I had never paid any particular attention to the few roses I bought, where I planted them or what happened to them. So most of them died, and when I got tired of seeing their withered brown skeletons, I just pulled them up and threw them into the garbage can.

One day, an acquaintance of mine, a writer, asked whether I would like some free roses. At first I declined, on the ground that my roses kept dying, but then I decided that a few more deaths wouldn't greatly matter. I asked him why he was distributing free roses.

"I was interviewing Pamela Travers," he said, "and she said she wished somebody would name a rose in her honor, so when the interview came out in the *Saturday Review,* I got a letter from a rose-grower, saying he'd named a rose for Mary Poppins, and did I know anybody who'd like some samples?"

I was in Europe when one of my children wrote me that four roses had arrived, and that the Mississippi cleaning woman who was then running the household had planted them at random points in the garden. Three of the four flourished, and put out salmon pink flowers, but they were not particularly handsome roses. Mary Poppins herself, of course, was no beauty. But I still find it a little odd that my first roses were of a kind I didn't want or plant or like. They are my stepchildren now, those Mary Poppinses, rather plain and quite unloved, but they bloom, for some reason, endlessly, indestructibly.

3.

P*eace*

The first rose that I actually chose for myself was a pink and yellow one called Peace. It was early in the spring, and I felt like buying flowers, and so I drove to the nursery to see what I could find. The nursery was almost bare, for it was still too early for potted roses to be set out in the April winds, but there was a row of dormant roots in cardboard boxes against one wall of the greenhouse. Each box showed a handsome picture of how the rose would someday look. The one called Peace looked large and handsome, and I liked its name.

At the time, I knew nothing of the stories that often lie behind the great roses. Peace, for instance, was the creation of a noted French horticulturist, Francis Meilland, who developed this new specimen during the dark days of 1942 in his nursery outside

Lyons, in what was then Unoccupied France. World War II was unpleasant, of course, but one gathers that such events, to a rosarian, are merely interruptions in the essential process of creating new kinds of roses.

In any case, Meilland named his new masterpiece after his mother, Madame Antoine Meilland. Then, unable to bear the idea of such a creation remaining confined within the limits of Vichy France, he persuaded the American consul in Lyons to smuggle the new rose back to America. Here, it was turned over to the Conard-Pyle Company, which took out a patent on behalf of Meilland—and also took the liberty of renaming his discovery. And so the flower that Meilland had dedicated to his mother was changed to Peace, and under that banner it became one of the best-selling roses of the whole postwar period. I was just one of the thousands who were attracted by the name, as well as the color, and I bought it. (In the former enemy countries, incidentally, there was equally little enthusiasm for Meilland's mother. German rose-growers renamed the plant Gloria Dei, and in Italy it became Gioia.)

But roses in cardboard boxes—in my experience, at least—don't grow very well. The main reason is that they have been sprayed with wax, to keep them alive during their long hibernation. I planted two boxes of Peace outside my living room window, and both plants struggled feebly into flower. The roses themselves were beautiful, a bright yellow tinged with pink at the tips, but that one flowering seemed to be all that these battered plants were destined to achieve. When the snow melted in the following March, they were both dead.

4.

Dappled things

The natural place to grow a real rose garden —in contrast to my sporadic planting of isolated roses —was in a sheltered and sun-dappled corner of the oak forest on the south side of my house. Every guide and handbook would have told me that I was wrong, because roses need a lot of sun, but I thought it would be more interesting to start the rose garden first and then to consult the guides afterwards. When I did, finally, they were quite explicit.

How to Grow Roses, by J. Horace McFarland and Robert Pyle, for example, has a section devoted to questions and answers. The first question is: "Will roses grow in shade?" The answer is: "No. They need at least five to six hours of direct sun each day."

I live in the woods, however, and there is no place in these woods that gets five to six hours of direct sun each day. The only way to get that much sun would be to cut down half a dozen oak trees, but the oak trees are what make this old place different from the standard Long Island split-level. And in due time, it becomes clear that the guidebooks are wrong. Roses can and will grow in the shade of the oak trees, not as strongly and brightly as they would in a field of sun, but that is not why I planted a rose garden in the first place.

> Glory be to God for dappled things—
> For skies of couple-colour as a brinded cow;
> For rose-moles all in stipple upon trout that swim;
> Fresh-firecoal chestnut-falls; finches' wings . . .

5.

Frau karl druschki

Every month or so, during that first summer, I went to the nursery and bought two more hybrid teas for my rose garden. Since I knew nothing about roses, I simply picked two that looked handsome and healthy. But their names were also important. It is not true that "a rose by any other name would smell as sweet." I like names that evoke the past, or far places, and I am inclined to pass by any plant called Lowell Thomas or Arlene Francis. One of the first roses I bought was tall and cream-white and bore the name of Matterhorn. When I took my wife to the nursery to join in picking another rose, she chose a pink and yellow blend called Tiffany. Then came—always just one of each kind—a series of red roses: Carrousel, and Scarlet Knight, and Etoile de Hollande, and Mister Lincoln. And a new Peace.

And Frau Karl Druschki. This is a beautiful white rose, of the type called Hybrid Perpetual, and I couldn't help wondering how it had acquired such a curiously ugly name. Who was Frau Karl Druschki? The wife of some dignitary, obviously, but what was her real name? Charlotte? Victoria? Eugenie? And what was she to the man who gave her name to this rose? I assumed for a time that the flower had been developed by Herr Druschki, but that was not the case. The creator was a man named Peter Lambert, who produced this new specimen in Germany in 1900 and named it for the wife of the president of the German Rose Society. Despite the forbidding name, Frau Karl Druschki soon became the favorite rose of King Edward VII, who liked to present clusters of these white flowers to the actresses he courted. But Frau Druschki herself? I see her quite clearly, a white-robed figure out of Degas, possibly of Polish origin, her long brown hair done up with combs, her gray eyes coolly intelligent—a woman never without admirers, but always faithful to her stout and white-bearded husband.

Despite all her virtues, Frau Druschki's unfortunate name has made her some enemies. Over the years, a number of sales-minded American rose-growers have attempted to obliterate the lady and to redesignate her flower as Snow Queen. Their attempt has achieved little success. After the better part of a century, how could anything with a Disneyland name like Snow Queen overwhelm the traditions inherent in every syllable of Frau Karl Druschki?

6.

My father

In middle age, I find myself, more and more often, acting out the role of my own father. I do not do this deliberately, but neither do I resist it—in other words, I do not act against my own nature simply in order to deny my inheritance. Every year, therefore, I become increasingly aware that I habitually use my father's gestures, his mannerisms of speech. I have even, like him, grown rather fat.

It was only after I had begun my rose garden, though, that I realized that my father, too, had always had a rose garden. One of his first moves, after buying a farm in Vermont in 1933, when I was four, was to plant a lawn outside the windows that overlooked the valley down to the gleaming Connecticut River, and then to line the far end of that lawn with a bed of roses. I had not really forgotten it, of course, but

I truly remembered it only in the act of recreating it.

There had been a stone wall behind his rose garden, and then a meadow sloping down the hill, where the Jersey heifers grazed in the summers and we skied in the winters, down to the sugar house in the woods, where we brought the sled tank full of maple sap and poured it into vats and boiled it into maple syrup. That is all different now. The barns burned to the ground in the mid-forties, and the maple trees have been cut down to make way for a new superhighway alongside the old Route 5, and at the bottom of the valley, the Connecticut River is full of dead fish, floating white-bellied down to the sea.

My father bought a new farm in New Hampshire, but I have never lived there, and, in fact, we don't see each other very much any more. I paid him a visit not long ago, however, and we went out and inspected his present rose garden. My father has learned all the lessons one learns in the course of a half century of gardening. His roses are planted fairly close together, in rich soil, in full sunlight, and so they all bloom profusely. But they didn't make any great impression on me. They lacked—what shall I say?— soul. They looked like rows of garden vegetables.

My father is quite deaf nowadays, at the age of seventy, and so it is difficult to carry on any sort of conversation. One shouts at him, and he pretends to hear, but he often changes the subject to disguise the fact that he has heard almost nothing. He has also become very conservative, exasperated at all the disturbers of the peace, and so it is best not to talk about the state of the world. Instead, I follow him through his rose garden, listening to his observations on mulching and pruning, shouting back an occasional observation of my own. The roses give us something to talk about, or pretend to talk about. And I know that someday I shall lead my daughters through my own garden, listening to their conversational cries, and pretending that I can hear them.

🌹 7.

S *tones*

In the beginning, my rose garden had no plan and no shape. Having started by planting a red rose and a white rose in the middle of the woods, I deliberately left all the surrounding area as it was, partly because I didn't feel like doing a lot of digging and raking, partly because the very act of defining the work to be done might prevent me from ever undertaking it. This state of artificial innocence could not last for long. Two roses blooming in the middle of the woods can create the effect of a happy surprise, but six or eight roses blooming in the woods simply look neglected.

At about this same time, a series of summer rains made the dirt road leading up the hill almost impassable. Not only did the rains create deep gullies but they left the road clogged with dozens of loose stones.

It suddenly occurred to me that the anarchy in the driveway might resolve the anarchy of the rose garden —like a peaceful fusion of matter and antimatter— and so I spent the better part of a day carrying stones from the driveway to the rose garden and half burying them in a circumscribing trench.

The effect was extraordinary. The rose garden—a term I had hitherto used with a kind of self-deprecatory tone, as though the words were to be forever confined within quotation marks—suddenly became, in fact, a rose garden. The half-buried stones began almost immediately to look as though they had been implanted by some eccentric ancestor in the previous century, and the ragged line of gray-white humps provided what I had thought I did not want (but really did want)—a shape, a sense of order. For a long time, I stood and simply stared at the results of my work, my crooked row of stones, and I felt a surprisingly and mysteriously powerful sense of satisfaction at what I had done.

By what seemed an absurd coincidence, that same evening, I read a magazine article about the latest trend in sculpture, anno Domini 1968. Artists were tired of being confined within walls, the article said, and so they were creating their newest works outdoors, by various combinations of stones and earth patterns. One of them, named Mike Heizer, had actually been commissioned by a celebrated art patron to dig a 520-mile series of holes connecting eight dry lakes in the California desert. Another, Carl Andre, was engaged in heaping up pieces of sandstone. "These hunks of native stone are naturally occurring particles," the article quoted Andre as saying, with great solemnity, "which I simply display in a natural, unmodified manner."

That was the explanation, then, for my sense of satisfaction in regarding my array of rocks. I had not only created a rose garden but, according to the authorities, a work of art.

8.

Caterpillars

The first sign of the caterpillars, every spring, is a mysterious curling of the roses' new leaves. Inside each curled leaf, a cocoon shelters the infinitesimal green destroyer. Within a day or two, he is an inch long, and he has eaten the leaf that once sheltered him. Then he creeps up the stem toward a rosebud and starts gnawing into one side, digging himself into it. Within another day or two, the rosebud is a mutilated ruin.

I believe in poisoning pests—*pace* Rachel Carson and all those who cherish Dr. Schweitzer's "reverence for life"—and so I diligently spray my roses every week with chemicals that bear impressive names like rotenone, piperonyl butoxide, ferric dimethyldithiocarbamate, and triethanolamine oleate. This should, in theory, leave all the caterpillars writhing in agony beneath my flourishing roses. Unfortunately, my caterpillars seem to thrive on all the dread chemicals.

For about two weeks, during that first May, I waited for the poisoned caterpillars to die, and then I finally realized, as I surveyed the gnawed, tattered remnants of my rose garden, that I would have to do the killing myself. Catch the caterpillar between the fingers, drop it to the ground, and then step on it. Every morning, on every rose bush, I caught and killed half a dozen, and in the evenings, I sometimes killed half a dozen more. I speak of the matter coolly, but I found it a disgusting chore, and I found myself hating the squirming creatures I had to kill. And then, as suddenly as they had come, they vanished.

But I still wonder about the question that came to me as I caught and squashed these wriggling caterpillars: What purpose in God's universe could ever have inspired Him to create such things? The easy answer is that they provide food for birds, but I never saw any birds feeding on my caterpillars. And even if it was the caterpillars' destiny to be eaten—a destiny they never fulfilled—why must they, in the course of achieving their purpose, devote so much energy to ruining my roses?

Perhaps my mistake was to assume that the caterpillars were created to fulfill a function rather than simply to exist. And that mistake, in turn, derived from the fact that their desires conflicted with my own. Because I wanted to grow beautiful roses, and because the caterpillars wanted to eat them, I regarded the caterpillars as repulsive. But suppose that the caterpillars themselves had been created purely as objects of beauty. Is there any other animal more lithe, more graceful, more perfectly suited to its own destiny? And is the green and furry skin of the caterpillar intrinsically any less beautiful than the leaf of a rose? Suppose, then, that the only function of the rose, the basic reason for its existence, is to provide food for the magnificent caterpillar.

9.

Weeding

The garden manuals all advise mulching roses in the spring. By covering the ground with a layer of straw or bark or coconut fibers, they say, we enable the earth to retain its moisture, and we spare ourselves the trouble of weeding. There are drawbacks, though. One is that no mulch can ever be as handsome as plain earth. Instead of looking at a garden, we have to look at a bed of mulch. Besides, I rather like weeding.

In my childhood, it was the most hated of chores, partly because it never got finished, partly because it lacked all status. The older people did the glamorous work, like plowing or harrowing, from which one could also gain the satisfaction of a job well done. The youngest children, on the other hand, were handed hoes and sent out to attack the endless rows of green beans. We did it only on command, and for money, and my father's pay scale was low even for the Depression: five cents an hour.

In my own rose garden, however, weeding is quite different. It is a process of cleansing and purification, and after a morning's labor, the earth is once again immaculate. It has been cared for. Cared for—the words themselves are oddly ambiguous, implying either labor or affection, implying that the two meanings are interdependent. The beauty of a garden is not purely esthetic—or rather, we attach esthetic value to those aspects of a garden that bespeak labor. The neatly clipped privet hedge, the impeccable lawn, the well-tended apple orchard, these all please the eye because they imply the imposition of order on nature, and thus they have a beauty that would be lacking in such disorderly counterparts as a honeysuckle thicket, a meadow, or a grove of maple saplings. And when the labor that imposed order was our own, then we view the results not just with esthetic satisfaction but with real affection. It is by weeding, in short, that we begin to overcome one of the great sins of modern life, which is numbness, and to regard the world around us with genuine feeling.

There is another salutary element in weeding, and that is the position in which it places the weeder. I know of just two other tasks that require one to be on one's knees—prayer and floor scrubbing—and both of these, too, have their edifying aspects. It is only out-of-doors, though, that one gains a wholly new perspective by working on one's knees. In the rose garden, pulling up tufts of grass and chickweed, I sense, more than anywhere else, the closeness, the richness, the fertility, and the vast, solid mass of the earth itself.

🌹 10.

G*raduation*

The moment of triumph finally occurred one sunny day in the middle of June. I took a lady out to see my year-old rose garden, and instead of having to apologize for it, I simply waved an arm, in the manner of an impresario. I had planned the garden, in fact, so that strangers would come on it by surprise. As one approaches, along the path, everything is hidden behind a gigantic rhododendron, and then there it is. Some thirty different roses all in bloom—*voilà!*

As it happened, this was the day of my oldest daughter's graduation from high school, and so the house was filled with relatives, maidens in white dresses, and frog-voiced suitors. The centerpiece for the lunch was a magnificent salmon, which arrived, boned and skinned, with some imitation roses carved out of radishes, and a bill for twenty dollars. On the piano stood a vase full of red roses and ferns that one of the suitors had ordered shipped from a florist. Outside, in the woods, my garden was left to grow in unseen splendor.

11.

The smell of raspberries

All too often, when I take a visitor out to see my roses, I watch her bend over a large and beautiful flower, and then—I suppose I could let her struggle for the appropriate words, but I feel an obligation to inform her that there is nothing to smell. A kind of sensual evisceration has taken place. Some of my most handsome roses—Scarlet Knight, for example, or the superb white Pascali—have been bred for strength and appearance, at the expense of the smell that has bewitched people through the years.

"One *can* breed for fragrance, of course," says the voice of progress and commerce, in the form of Sam McGredy, head of a great nursery in Northern Ireland, "but on the way so many other good characteristics are lost. From a practical point of view, roses grown on a large scale, such as in parks and in large gardens, are admired for their visual effect rather than their scent."

The sense of smell is one of our most peculiar attributes, one of the most basic but least practical of our animal senses. Smells derive, apparently, from infinitesimal particles that become trapped in the mucous membrane in the upper part of the nose, and sensitive nerves in that membrane convey a sensory message to the brain. But once this mechanistic explanation is accepted, it remains difficult to understand why some smells seem so pleasant and others so unpleasant. I recently asked a number of people to list their favorite smells, and the answers were remarkably similar—newly mown grass, baking bread, wood shavings, apples and applesauce, burning leaves, seaweed or sea air or, more basically, the sea itself, and, of course, roses.

But there really is no such thing as a smell of roses. Some of them, as I have said, have no smell at all. Others have a smell that is distinctly unpleasant, sweet and rather tawdry. When I first found that one of my yellow roses had this affliction, I was startled by the very idea of a rose that smelled bad, and so I tried to figure out what makes some roses smell better than others. It is a question that has puzzled people for centuries, and the effort to classify rose scents goes back as far as Herodotus. In modern times, horticulturists have catalogued six distinct kinds of rose smells: damask scent, tea scent, fruit scent, musk scent, spice scent, and miscellaneous scents.

In my own garden, I lack such wide variety, or else I am unable to make such distinctions. But I found that the two best rose smells bear a definite resemblance to the smells of very different plants. One kind, which the official listing above calls "spice scent," is basically the smell of a lemon. The other, which appears on the official list as "fruit scent," is, I think, the smell of raspberries. Now as to the question of why a rose should smell like a raspberry, and why the smell of a raspberry should strike me as delightful, I have no answer. Or is it that raspberries taste delicious because they smell like the finest roses? Or do they both share some common origin for which we do not even have a name?

✿ 12.

Communication

James Gould Cozzens has written that roses must always be planted in clusters. "It was my mother's practice to plant together at least three of a kind," Cozzens said. "This ought of course to be everyone's practice. Dealers should refuse to sell less than three. A single bush . . . will not show off its blooms to best advantage. I know no good reasons why this should be so, but so it is."

In my rose garden, I have followed exactly the opposite principle, permitting only one rose of any kind, so that each plant would provide a contrast to all the others around it. Such eccentric theories are difficult to explain to large nurseries, and so, when I ordered three different roses from Jackson & Perkins, I got back two of the same kind, along with a computer's announcement that the third kind had been sold out.

The duplicates were a relatively new variety, a tall, bushy red rose called Proud Land. I put one of them in my rose garden and banished the other to a spot outside the kitchen. There it got more sun than my other roses; there it got spraying, fertilizer, and water, and there it slowly and inexorably began to turn yellow and die.

I was puzzled by its death, but one of my children offered the obvious explanation: "It was lonely."

That sounds absurd, of course, for we always assume that no organism can have any intellectual perceptions unless those perceptions are approximately the same as our own. But as I watched this isolated rose bush die, even though its physical circumstances were better than those that prevailed in the rose garden, I began to wonder why we take it for granted that plants have less sensibility than animals. Shortly after that, I discovered that the same kind of doubt had occurred almost a century ago to Samuel Butler.

"Most plants show unmistakable hostility to the animal world," Butler wrote. "They scratch, cut, prick, sting, make bad smells, secrete the most dreadful poisons. . . . If, on the other hand, they think an animal can be of use to them, they will coax it by every artifice in their power. . . . Whenever I hear a man say that a thing which manages its affairs with so keen an eye to the main chance as a nettle or a blackberry, has no intelligence and does not understand its own business, on the ground that it shows no sign of understanding ours, I always feel that however little intelligence the plant may have the man has even less."

13.

R*avens*

The rose garden lies at the upper edge of the woods, and although I have cut a path through the trees down to the street, the lands on the far side of that path are not wholly mine. The title deed does declare that the woods belong to me, but this claim is disputed by a dozen ravens. They perch in the broken tops of two dead oak trees. Whenever I come to look at my roses, the ravens squawk in protest—and in warning, to each other, and to me.

Alfred Hitchcock succeeded, in a perverse way, in achieving the goal of every artist: changing our perception of the world. After seeing *The Birds,* I can never again consider any of these creatures completely harmless. On the contrary, when the ravens start their cawing, I shudder and look warily up into the dead oaks, feeling that it would be best for me to know exactly where the birds are. The ravens were never innocent little sparrows, of course. When they flap from branch to branch, they reveal a wingspan of a yard or more, and there is something undeniably sinister about the blackness of their wings, the yellow of their beaks and eyes. I remember that ravens sat and cawed on the top of Breughel's gibbet, and that Villon's hanged men knew these birds would pick at their swaying corpses.

> La pluye nous a buez et lavez,
> Et le soleil desechez et noircis;
> Pies, corbeaulx, nous ont les yeux cavez,
> Et arraché la barbe et les sourcilz.
> Jamais, nul temps, nous ne sommes assis;
> Puis çà, puis là, comme le vent varie,
> A son plaisir sans cesser nous charie,
> Plus becquetez d'oiseaulx que dez à couldre.

"The thing to do is just shoot them," said a neighbor, a gray-haired but fiercely athletic lawyer with a large office in New York.

"We could even serve them in a pie," I answered. "If you could serve four and twenty blackbirds baked in a pie, why not a raven pie?"

"Exactly," said the lawyer. "But there's a trick to it. You have to get a stuffed owl, and you set that up in an open place, and then the ravens all come swooping down to attack it, and then you take your gun and just pop them off."

"And that's how you make a raven pie."

"Right!"

I was joking, but the gray-haired lawyer was not. He really believed in using a stuffed owl as a trap, and he really would have liked to kill all the ravens. In theory, I would like to kill them too, but I will never do anything about them, except to curse them.

🌹 14.

Chrysanthemums

For almost a year, I watched the chrysanthemums grow in various corners of my rose garden. They had been planted there by the previous owner of the house, who treated this area as a sort of auxiliary garden, fit for experiments and leftovers. About a dozen of her chrysanthemums still survived, coppery brown and rather spindly, and I could not bring myself to destroy them. Did Dr. Schweitzer's "reverence for life" apply to plants, or just to ants and beetles?

But this is sentimentality and amateurishness. In a garden, all weeds must die. In a rose garden, a chrysanthemum is a weed. So I pulled them up and flung them into the woods.

🌹 15.

A few pieces of history

"A rose is a rose is a rose," said Gertrude
Stein, but it is not true. Most of the roses now being
sold to American gardeners were developed only during the last few years, and the roses that appear in
Shakespeare (or, for that matter, in Virgil) are quite
different from the standard suburban variety.

The traditional rose was a shrub, with rather small
but strongly scented flowers, which bloomed profusely
once a year. The only exception was a type known as
Autumn Damask, *Rosa damascena bifera,* a cross between the original *Rosa gallica* and *Rosa moschata,*
developed in Greece as early as the tenth century
B.C. This rose was greatly valued because it flowered
twice, and so it spread throughout the Mediterranean
world. Not until the middle of the eighteenth century, however, did a Scandinavian voyager discover,

in the customshouse garden in Canton, a pink rose that flowered all summer. And with the coming of the fragile but everblooming China roses, there began a century of botanical crossing and recrossing, an international process of hybridization that soon grew complicated beyond all telling.

To take just a few examples in the development of the hybrid tea rose: Sir Joseph Banks, director of Kew Gardens, and a companion of Captain Cook on his first tour around the world, brought back to England in about 1790 a pink China rose, which ended on the estate of a Mr. Parsons in Hertfordshire. For some reason that is not entirely clear, Parsons' Pink China rose was planted together with some Autumn Damask roses as a windbreak on the French island of Bourbon, now known as Réunion, a volcanic pinpoint 400 miles southeast of Madagascar. Here the two roses mated by themselves, producing an everblooming hybrid that attracted the attention of a visiting French horticulturist, who sent the new "Bourbon rose" back to the garden of the Duc d'Orleans at the Chateau de Neuilly, just outside Paris.

During this same period, another British horticulturist named Gilbert Slater brought to England another everblooming China rose, a low-growing red one, which acquired the name of Slater's Crimson China rose, and which, in an Italian garden, mated naturally with other varieties and produced a new type, and this, in turn, came to the attention of the visiting Duchess of Portland, who took it back to England as the first Portland Rose.

Now, the Portland Rose mated with the Bourbon Rose, in 1816, at the French royal gardens at Sèvres, and that produced the first Hybrid Perpetual, an everblooming red flower named Rose du Roi. During the succeeding years, another development from the China roses produced the Noisette rose, and the Noisette, when combined with another Chinese strain, produced the classic Tea rose. And finally, in 1867, a French rose-grower combined a richly scented tea rose named Madame Bravy with one of the tougher hybrid perpetuals named Madame Victor Verdier and created the first specimen of the standard modern rose, the Hybrid Tea. It was called, naturally enough, La France.

Only a century ago, then, the hybrid tea rose was a strange new creation, produced by the same kind of scientific inventiveness that was developing the textile mill and the steam railroad. But rose-growers have never been technocrats, and so it was quite fitting that the first rose show in London was organized in 1858 by S. Reynolds Hole, Dean of Rochester, and author of the classic *A Book About Roses*. "I feel no shame in confessing," Dean Hole wrote later, "that when the hall was cleared and I looked from the gallery upon the three long tables . . . glowing with the choicest Roses in the world, the cisterns of my heart overflowed."

16.

D*ean hole's guide to salvation*

"The cisterns of my heart." That is fairly typical of the euphuistic prose and no less euphuistic passions of Dean Hole. He is often quoted in other books on roses—for he was an authentic expert, as well as a charming figure of his time—but it is not easy to find an actual copy of *A Book About Roses.* My wife ordered it from England as a Christmas present, but December had become June before I finally received a battered, rust-red volume, the twenty-sixth edition, published in 1910.

"He who would have beautiful Roses in his garden," says Dean Hole in his very first sentence, "must have beautiful Roses *in his heart.* He must love them well and always. To win, he must woo, as Jacob wooed Laban's daughter, though drought and frost consume. . . ."

One can see immediately that Dean Hole is no ordinary gardener, and no ordinary writer about the pleasures of gardening. He speaks with lordly contempt of the rich man who tries to show him "one of those dismal slaughter-houses which he calls his Rosary," and when the rich man complains of his expensive failures, Dean Hole answers by saying, "You have taken no trouble which deserves the name; and as to expense, permit me to observe that your fifty Rose-trees did not cost you a fifth of the sum which you paid for your sealskin jacket. You don't deserve beautiful Roses. . . ." When, on the other hand, Dean Hole finds some humble workmen who have grown masterpieces on tiny plots of land, he marvels at their dedication. "How was it done?" he asks. *"De l'abondance du coeur. . . ."*

From such observations, Dean Hole draws far-reaching conclusions. "I have always believed," he says, "that the happiness of mankind may be increased by encouraging that love of a garden, that love of the beautiful, which is innate in us all. Get a man out of the dram and beer shops into the fresh pure air, interest him in the marvellous works of his God, instead of in the deformities of vice, give him an occupation which will add to his health and the comforts of his family, instead of destroying both, then build Revealed upon Natural Religion, and hope to see him a Christian."

17.

O*ld roses*

The best of the modern hybrid tea roses and floribundas come from the large nurseries like Jackson & Perkins, Conard-Pyle, or Armstrong, and each new specimen is patented and heavily advertised, all of which helps to keep the prices high. But what ever became of all those old roses that flower in English poetry? What happened to the Portland rose and the Bourbon rose and the original version of Slater's Crimson China rose?

There is a large and cheerful-looking woman who has made the answers to these questions her function in life, and so, in due time, we meet Mrs. Dorothy Stemler, of Brown's Valley Road in Watsonville, California. About thirty years ago, she went to work as a secretary for a citrus-fruit grower named Will Tillotson, who, on his retirement, started a plantation devoted to the reproduction of what are known as Old Roses. When Tillotson died, Mrs. Stemler inherited the business, which now produces 90,000 roses, of 200 varieties, every year. But Mrs. Stemler is no mere plantation owner; she is an enthusiast, a missionary, and the author of one of the most engaging catalogues in the business. It includes not only her effusive description of each Old Rose but her own photographs of them, her "random thoughts," a portrait of her dog, and a variety of horticultural quotations from Goethe, Lin Yutang, Ralph Waldo Emerson, and Wilbur C. Munnecke.

Finding this kind of obsession engaging, I ordered four of Mrs. Stemler's Old Roses. I started with a Hybrid China rose that had been introduced in 1897 under the name of Grüss an Teplitz—meaning Greetings to Teplitz—Teplitz being the German name for a spa that is now called Teplice, in Czechoslovakia—and the only reason I selected this oddity was that Mrs. Stemler's catalogue informed us that Grüss an Teplitz had featured in James Gould Cozzens' solemnly celebrated novel, *By Love Possessed*. It was a very brief and ambiguous accolade, as I learned on checking back through Cozzens' novel: Arthur Winner, the prudish hero, was showing his rose garden to a rather forward visitor named Mrs. Pratt. " 'That's Gruss an Teplitz,' Arthur Winner said. . . . 'What heavenly fragrance!' With a supple enough, smooth-membered swaying forward, all those ripe curvatures of form dropping pendent in their wrappings, Mrs. Pratt buried her nose in a blossom. She gave Arthur Winner, over it, a liquid ecstatic up-glance. . . ."

If anyone like Mrs. Pratt ever came to visit me, then, I would be ready for her. And for places of honor alongside Grüss an Teplitz, I ordered three more roses with the most aristocratic of names—a hybrid perpetual (1861) called Prince Camille de Rohan ("A handsome and richly perfumed prince of roses, dressed in royal velvet!" cried Mrs. Stemler); a tea rose (1857) called Duchesse de Brabant ("Teddy Roosevelt's favorite rose!" said Mrs. Stemler); and an older hybrid perpetual (1839) named Baronne Prevost ("One of the earliest, one of the finest and most prolific. My favorite. . . .").

It would be pleasant to report that the Old Roses proved to be better than any modern rose, that the Old Roses are still finer and more fragrant than the bigger and stronger products of modern technology. Unfortunately, I did not find it so. Three of the four prospered, but their flowers were rather small, and the famous "old-rose fragrance" turned out to be very mild. The only one that was truly unusual was the Duchesse de Brabant, which produced four or five beautiful pink flowers and really did give off the smoky smell of an old tea chest. It was a rather weak plant, though, and the roses drooped on their stems, and I had difficulty in visualizing the Duchesse as the favorite of Teddy Roosevelt. The president's summer home, Sagamore Hill, is only a few miles from here, and I have occasionally gone to marvel at his collection of moose heads and tiger skins, and the elephant legs that have been hollowed out to hold walking sticks and umbrellas. The Duchesse de Brabant was never conceived on such a scale, and after producing her half-dozen pink flowers, she inexorably faded and died.

My mistake, I think, was in ordering plants that were just a little older and just a little more resonant than the standard nursery fare. What folly, in retrospect, to compete with the twentieth century by conjuring up the flowers of the nineteenth, what folly to plant the favorite rose of Teddy Roosevelt when I could be planting the favorite rose of Virgil. This spring, I am replacing the Duchesse de Brabant, because I think that all dead roses should be replaced, but I am going beyond that. Send me *Rosa gallica officinalis,* Mrs. Stemler, the one described in your catalogue as the Apothecary Rose that flourished in Provence in the thirteenth century; send me *Rosa damascena bifera,* the one that the Romans heaped on the altars of Venus, the one that Cleopatra used to cushion the floors for Antony. Send me the roots and seeds of our civilization, Mrs. Stemler, for which I enclose a check for $5.50, plus $1.50 for shipping charges.

18.

Garbage roses

Long after I had planted my rose garden, my wife complained about its location. It was too far from the house, she said, and it could never be seen from a window. I answered that a garden was not a back porch, not an extension of the house, but rather a place by itself, to be visited and enjoyed on its own terms. Every classic designer, I went on, had argued that a garden should never be visible all at once. It should be a series of happy surprises, of views and vistas leading to new views and vistas.

From the consequent silence, I knew that my argument had had no effect whatever.

"All right," I said, "where would you like to have a rose planted?"

"There," my wife promptly answered, pointing through the kitchen window at the three battered garbage cans that stood next to the garage. "That's what I have to look at every day."

Well why not? I thought. If the littered ground next to a garbage can is the spot where a rose will be best seen and most enjoyed, then that's where a rose should be. On one side of the garbage cans, nowadays, there grows a climbing pink New Dawn, and on the other side a red climber named Don Juan. They too, in their way, provide a classic garden design.

❧ 19.

Number 58-6103

Four of my roses have no names at all, only numbers. This is because I received an invitation from Jackson & Perkins to become a member of the company's "test panel." For only $12.00, not much less than the company's regular price for its best sellers, I could become one of ten thousand customers in the "special group" to sign up for four "experimental" roses, types that had never been put on sale, or even named. And at the end of the summer, I would send the company my personal report on how the new plants fared. I knew that Jackson & Perkins didn't really attach any great weight to my views—the company proclaims that it markets only one in ten thousand seedlings developed by its research department, and that each new specimen on the market represents an investment of $50,000 and up to ten years' time—but the appeal to my vanity was too strong to resist.

It took a little time for me to realize that my four new roses were something less than a bargain—not because of the price, which was standard, but because of the quality of the plants. Was there any reason, after all, to think that Jackson & Perkins had discovered some magic new formula? Or to doubt that the best roses were probably those that had already passed the tests we were about to impose on their successors?

My new roses were named, respectively, No. 8131, No. 8167, No. 8282, and No. 58-6103. The first three turned out, as I had come to expect, quite unremarkable, but No. 58-6103 proved to be an extraordinary plant. For one thing, it was very strong and sturdy, shooting up within a few weeks to a height of more than four feet. With all its strength, it was eager to flower. It produced bud after bud, each one perfectly formed, each one a bright lemon yellow, each one filled with a powerful smell. One didn't need to poke one's nose into No. 58-6103 to receive its offerings; they became obvious at a distance of two or three feet.

The trouble was that the smell of No. 58-6103 was not a very pleasant smell. It was too sweet, too cloying, too reminiscent of something or other. I tried for a time to think what No. 58-6103 reminded me of, and then it suddenly came to me—the cosmetics counter at F. W. Woolworth's in Brattleboro, Vermont. It was simply the smell of cheap perfume. And those beautiful yellow buds had a problem too. They had absolutely no endurance. Within two days after each flower had opened, the petals would flutter to the ground, leaving behind, all exposed, the reproductive system. What No. 58-6103 was, in short, was a rosarian version of the wanton shopgirl in the late nineteenth-century novel.

Jackson & Perkins sent me a set of evaluation forms, which the company said had been simplified for submission to the computer. All that a member of the "test panel" had to do was to check whether a numbered rose had proven to be excellent, good, fair, or poor in such categories as "disease resistance" and "floriferousness." One was also invited to submit names, like Pink Glory, Yellow Cloud, and so on. I rebelled against the computer form and sent Jackson & Perkins a long letter (which the computer never answered) describing the six months I had spent with my nameless protégés.

I described in considerable detail the unusual character of No. 58-6103, its reckless growth, its transitory beauty, its thick but vulgar perfume, its foolish optimism. I did not, however, tell Jackson & Perkins my theory about the yellow rose's proletarian personality, nor did I offer to name it. Only now, in fact, do the proper names come to mind. It should be named after Somerset Maugham's Mildred Rogers, or Sister Carrie, or possibly even Nana. But now I always think of her as No. 58-6103.

🌹 20.

*P*redecessors

One of the pleasures of buying an old house is that one inherits the results of other people's work in the garden. Here I have a marvelous bed of crocuses that somebody else planted in a sheltered spot just below a garden wall. Here I have a grand assortment of somebody else's laurel bushes and somebody else's mountainous rhododendron.

I wish, though, that I knew more about the four rambler rose bushes that sprawl over a wooden fence at the northern edge of the garden, or about the dark red rose that twines around a thick post outside my study window. I wrote to the woman from whom I bought the house, and she recalled having planted a few roses down the hill, though she couldn't remember their names. But the big bushes that froth into bloom every July, she doesn't know where they came from, who planted them, or what their names are. They were here when she came to the house, and here when she left it. I wonder whether the same will some day be true for me.

21.

The cherry orchard

To one side of the rose garden stands a dead cherry tree, a sapling about three feet high, its branches neatly pruned, and all quite lifeless. Visitors from the city occasionally express bewilderment at the existence of such a piece of wooden statuary in the middle of a garden.

"What's that?" The question is always phrased the same way.

"It's a dead cherry tree," I answer.

The visitor never asks why a dead cherry tree stands beside the rose garden, and so I never explain.

When we first moved to Long Island, fifteen years ago, we rented a small colonial house framed by two wind-whipped apple trees. Eventually, we bought an old house of our own, again surrounded by apple trees, and here we learned that our former house had been bulldozed to make room for a parking lot next to the new supermarket, and here I planted two pear trees, two hazelnut trees, a cherry, and a holly. The bulldozers eventually reached us again, knocking down the twenty-foot lilac and the privet hedge that lined the street, then demolishing the woods on the other side of the street—all for the purpose of widening the highways that brought people from New York City to Jones Beach. We moved again, to the North Shore, and again I planted fruit trees, starting with two Baldwin apple trees and two Bing cherry trees, along the path that bordered an empty space where no rose garden yet existed. The apple trees survived, but the cherry trees proved more fragile than I had thought. Weakened first by caterpillars and then by drought, they succumbed during their first summer.

I suppose there is something very Germanic about this struggle to raise fruit trees in the path of the bulldozer—"Even if I knew the world would end tomorrow," Martin Luther once said, "I would continue to plant my apple trees"—but the most eloquent version of my story was written by a Russian. When I first saw *The Cherry Orchard,* I marveled at Chekhov's determination to make the doomed trees represent something more than trees. "Oh, my childhood, my innocence!" cried Madame Ranevsky as she recalled what the orchard had meant to her. But the voice that sounded most familiar to me was that of Lopahin, the merchant: "If the cherry orchard and the land along the river bank were cut up into building plots and then let on lease for summer villas, you would make an income of at least 250,000 roubles a year out of it." The play ends, of course, with the sound of the axe echoing offstage, and there is nothing metaphorical about it. What Chekhov was writing was quite literally the story of Long Island.

I left my dead cherry tree standing by the rose garden, therefore, partly as an ornament (for it was, despite its deadness, a handsome thing), partly as a monument to past failures, and partly as a reminder of work to be done. To combat Lopahin's bulldozers, I needed not one or two saplings but a whole orchard. I sent a check to a nursery in Tennessee and got back eight young cherry trees, four Montmorency and four Black Tartarian—not enough to replace all the giant oaks that will eventually die and fall, but enough to make a beginning.

🌹 22.

T he american rose society

All obsessions are organized, in this country, and so I duly joined the American Rose Society, 4048 Roselea Place, Columbus, Ohio 43214, a city that boasts a municipal rose garden of 35,000 plants, and thus claims the title of rose capital of the world.

My main purpose was to acquire the Society's _Handbook for Selecting Roses,_ in which every standard plant receives a rating on a scale from one to ten, but I was also interested in getting some idea of what a national rose society actually does. For my annual dues of $7.50 (the fee subsequently went up to $10.50, despite the vehement protests of the elderly members, who demanded that the Society's annual expenses of $180,000 be drastically reduced), I began receiving the Society's monthly magazine, _The American Rose._

I had thought that such a magazine might bring me a regular compendium of advice on the respective merits of various new fertilizers, but the only information of this kind appeared in a regular feature entitled Uncle Charlie's Corner. Uncle Charlie, a bespectacled gentleman with a large smile, was identified as Charles P. Dawson, of Finchville, Kentucky, and he made it a practice to express his opinions in a Finchville vernacular ("Things are getting better all the time, I'll tell ya. We have been trying a new wrinkle in rose garden layout. And, by doggies, everyone likes it, I think. . . .")

The Society and its magazine devoted relatively little attention to rural wisdom of this sort, however. At its most scholarly level, the Society took pride in the activities of the American Rose Foundation, which it described as "a non-profit trust dedicated to research for the improvement of roses." In the annual report of the Research Committee, therefore, Dr. Cynthia Wescott announced benefactions like the award of $1,000 to the department of horticulture at the University of Iowa, where "the study of understock-scion incompatibility resulting from necrotic tissue formation has continued." On a less exalted level, the Society also offered its members rose-decorated tie clips ($3.00), key holders ($2.50), charms ($2.00), or bumper stickers (30 cents each, or four for $1.00).

Most of the Society's efforts, however, seemed to

be devoted to the planning and recording of an endless series of meetings and conventions—with endless photographs of people in gray hair and gray suits smiling cheerfully as they presented awards to one another—and that was how I first encountered the name of Lester E. Satterlee, of Kansas City, Missouri. Mr. Satterlee, president of the Society, looked a bit like Barry Goldwater, with a strong jaw, back-swept gray hair, and horn-rimmed glasses, and his monthly message to the members was one of tireless enthusiasm. "The American Rose Society is on the move," Mr. Satterlee announced at one point. "Doesn't that sound great? Our membership is up over 500 members from what it was a year ago. All systems are go."

Going and moving appeared to be the principal themes of Mr. Satterlee's presidency. In its issue of May, 1969, *The American Rose* devoted its cover (a handsome photograph of a lion on a rock) to a story on the American Rose Society's "Rose Tour of Africa." For a payment of only $2,000 each, a group of up to 100 rosarians would spend three weeks touring the gardens of Africa, a tour which, except for a three-day safari from the Nairobi Hilton, consisted almost entirely of visits to the gardens of the Union of South Africa, notably the Kirstenbosch Gardens in Capetown and the Emmerentia Rose Garden in Johannesburg. "For those making plans for 1971," Mr. Satterlee also reported, "the International Rose Convention is to be held in the 2nd week of November at Hamilton, New Zealand. Doug Butcher, President of the National Rose Society of New Zealand, says they are . . . leaving no stones unturned to give you all a good time."

In between such major expeditions, Mr. Satterlee went on more limited safaris, generally accompanied by his wife, Bea. The regular "President's message" in the June issue, for instance, began with the announcement that "The Houston National Convention has passed into history. . . . Thanks, Houstonians—invite us back again some time; it was great." A mere convention, however, was not enough to keep the president fully occupied. "Bea and I took a side trip to Midland, Texas, on the way back," his report continued. "What a terrific group they have there in West Texas. . . . They did present me with three oil wells (on a tie–cuff link set), and Bea with a horned toad. Thanks, Midland, you were wonderful."

A couple of years have passed since then, other enthusiasts have succeeded to the presidency of the American Rose Society, and I, burdened with other chores, have allowed my subscription to *The American Rose* to lapse. But I have always missed the rich, floribunda prose of Lester Satterlee, who concluded his 1968 report by announcing "one thing we should not

lose sight of—the fact that this is a fun organization."
Well said, Mr. Satterlee, and thanks to you, and to
your courageous wife, Bea. I still wonder sometimes
what she said when the good ladies of Midland,
Texas, presented her with that horned toad.

🌹 23.

January

Somebody with a peculiar sense of humor gave me a Venus fly-catcher for Christmas. The most unnatural of plants, it came buried in a sort of brown plastic mulch, contained in a white plastic pot, and covered by a transparent plastic bag. An accompanying set of instructions dwelled at unseemly length on the plant's carnivorous appetites. I gave it some water and put it on a shelf, where, as I hoped, it died.

Outside, the roses stand serene in a hostile field of ice and snow. One of them, Peace, still holds a flower that grew in November but never opened. It has faded from yellow to a grandmotherly brown. The field of ice gives one a sense of death, speckled by beagle tracks, but the roses are alive. Each of them has at least a dozen tiny buds pushing outward from the stalks. The buds, red and new, look as though they hurt.

🌹 24.

W^{ishes}

I wish my rose garden had a more formal style—not so precious as the Japanese nor so arid as the French—but with less of the wildness of a wind-blown *jardin anglais*. I wish I had a brick wall—I wish that, like Churchill in his early retirement, I could build it myself. Unfortunately, I am not Churchill. All I have done is to buy a bench, a white iron bench—and that is primarily for convenience. Next, I suppose, I could buy a statue of some sort. I'd like something supremely banal—a stone angel or a nymph—but the garden isn't really large enough to make up for such lapses in taste.

What I miss most, I think, is water. A fountain would be grand, but even that would be only a beginning. A perfect rose garden should have not just fountains but ponds and moats and waterfalls, all designed to frame or mirror the beauty of the flowers. If only I were André Malraux and had Versailles as my planting site, I might achieve something interesting.

25.

C^{alvary}

My wife does not really like the rose garden. I have a theory to explain this: She sees everything outdoors from the viewpoint of the kitchen window, and everything that can be seen from the kitchen becomes an extension of her house, like the garbage roses, while everything else remains forever alien. Her own theory, however, is simply that my rose garden has too much the quality of a battlefield. With its forest soil and its perpetual shade, it will never produce the luxuriant flowering that occurs on even the most neglected estates of England or Ireland. Its plants will flower only thinly, and each one of those flowers will represent a victory in the struggle for life. I find that inspiring, but my wife does not.

"That isn't a garden," she once said. "It's a kind of Calvary."

26.

Spring

I used to recognize spring partly by the calendar, partly by the eruption of daffodils from the wet grass, partly by the announcements from the United States Government, warning me that it was time to pay tribute for the privilege of having survived another year.

Now the surest sign of spring is the transformation of the swollen rosebuds into the sprouting of green and red leaves. In November, just before the ground froze, each plant was buried under a pile of protective earth, and now it is time to clear away all of that debris, to prune away the dead wood, to give the renascent roses their first feeding, and to prepare for a new season of life.

✿ 27.

And all shall be well

It is clear that roses are more than just flowers. Or rather, as the most beautiful of all flowers, they seem to have a significance that is transcendental. They symbolize states of being that are beyond ordinary understanding. Although the symbolic quality of the rose is clear, however, it is much less clear what the rose actually symbolizes.

In classical times, the rose was primarily an emblem of love, and it had a religious significance largely because of its association with Aphrodite (Botticelli's painting shows the birth not only of the goddess but also of her flower, appearing simultaneously in the seas off Cyprus). In the early years of the Christian church, the authorities disapproved of the rose, as they disapproved of all the symbols of Aphrodite, but when the church became strong enough to absorb the old cults, it absorbed their symbols as well. The red rose, which once was said to have sprouted from the blood of the fallen Adonis, was now said to have sprouted from the thorns around the head of the crucified Jesus. The white rose became a symbol of the purity of both Jesus and the Virgin Mary.

Nothing is ever so simple, of course. The rose remained a symbol of love (hence the *Roman de la Rose*), and of ancient arcana (hence the tarot cards, based on the term *rota,* or wheel, which is both linguistically and symbolically connected to the rose). There was more than purely Christian imagery, therefore, in the magnificent rose windows of Chartres. And we can only share the awed bewilderment of Dante when he arrives at the end of his journey and finds himself confronting the symbolic manifestation of Paradise itself in the form of a gigantic yellow rose, "brighter than a million suns, immaculate, inaccessible, vast, fiery with magnificence, and surrounding God as if with a million veils."

We sense, in ways that we do not understand, that the rose represents many of the elements and conditions that we most profoundly cherish: beauty, love, purity, serenity, life itself, and even the transfiguration that passes beyond life. Yet when we attempt to analyze the meaning of any of these inadequate

words, we find only more words. And so, since I
began with "Burnt Norton," I shall end with "Little
Gidding":

> And all shall be well and
> All manner of thing shall be well
>
> . . . .
>
> When the tongues of flame are in-folded
> Into the crowned knot of fire
> And the fire and the rose are one.